AN ANGUISHED CRY FOR OUR ENDANGERED PLANET

Gladwin Das

ISBN: 1492775029
ISBN 13: 9781492775027
Library of Congress Control Number: 2013917723
CreateSpace Independent Publishing Platform
North Charleston, South Carolina

To all the children of the world.

Children are the most precious treasures that we possess. Everything we do and own, in a brief period of time, becomes a legacy passed on to our children. As we look at the sorry state of global affairs and the massive destruction of life-sustaining ecological systems, we the adults of this world need to ask ourselves two questions: Are we truly worthy of the world's wonderful children? How do we leave behind a planet that is worthy of our children and future generations?

CONTENTS

PREFACE

In 1991, during Operation Desert Storm, I watched the televised massive bombardment and explosions of a war being broadcast in living rooms all over the world. My son, who was four years old, was playing on the carpet with his toys. He stopped, looked at the television, and as he watched the bombs going off became extremely distressed. Running into my arms, he said, "Won't the bombs hurt, Papa?"

As I held him close to my heart, I asked myself, "Why does a four-year-old child have enough room in his heart for the entire world, yet we adults who manage its affairs cannot conduct ourselves in a manner truly worthy of them?" The issue for him was not the justification of that war or the unacceptable provocation that resulted in Operation Desert Storm. His impression—far more insightful and human—demonstrated the purity of a child's worldview. To a child, killing and hurting other humans should not be the way we manage our affairs.

The answer to that haunting question and several more that my growing son and daughter often asked of me, has resulted in this book. We must find a better way to manage global affairs and address major issues that face the species *Homo sapiens*. We must do so with a sense of urgency and purpose. Failure is not an acceptable option. Far too much is at stake.

I would like to start with a profound and sincere apology to anyone my book offends. I am not a man of letters, a diplomat, an expert in world affairs, a religious leader, or a philosopher. I am merely a physician. I see the world and all human beings from a very different perspective than most. I have spent my life comforting the sick and saving lives, and I have been privileged to touch the lives of thousands of my patients, their families, and friends. My patients are believers of all the major religions of the world. They range from the abjectly poor to the unimaginably wealthy, from many who cannot read or write to several brilliant intellectuals. I have been humbled to earn the gratitude and respect of this small sampling of humans that is representative of humans all over the world. I intend no critique to any religious, political, or racial group; I merely offer the perspective of a physician, who in the pursuit of truth sees human beings as one species with a common origin, a shared interrelated existence, and a common destiny.

As I cross the sixtieth year of my existence on this planet, it is obvious to me that my years ahead are definitely going to be fewer than the years I have lived. It is hence an age for reflection and thought. Everything that we do will soon be a legacy for our children. We will leave behind all our worldly possessions when we depart this planet, and all our contributions as well as misdeeds will pass on to future generations. We must reflect on how we can leave behind a legacy that we can all be proud of. The world is beset by seemingly insurmountable problems: from horrendous, barbaric violence fueled by religious, political, racial, tribal, and ethnic differences to the rapid destruction of life-sustaining ecological systems on earth. We can be apathetic to these problems or find tangible ways to collectively address them. How do we achieve this worthy goal?

The only way to move the human race to an enlightened existence is to start by putting our strong, protective, collective arms around the world's children. Every child is a precious jewel, irrespective of religion, nationality, or ethnic group. They are tender saplings who need to be nurtured to grow into peace-loving, productive world citizens. Can we look beyond our differences and see what binds us together as a species? Can we transform our fundamental approach to each other and to critical global problems that must be tackled with a sense of urgency?

I have dug deep within my being and have asked myself seemingly impossible to answer questions. On several weighty questions, mere humans cannot provide answers. How do we reconcile the irreconcilable? How do we build bridges between nations and religions, not walls of suspicion and hatred? Our ability to look at all issues with profound humility must be the first step. A path of humility and mutual respect that leads to a peaceful, productive coexistence is critical to our capacity to tackle major problems that threaten not only our long-term survival but that of all life forms on this beautiful planet.

It is time to look at solutions from a global human perspective. We are the species *Homo sapiens*. We are one. We owe it to our children and future generations to discover our oneness as a species and leave behind a legacy worthy of them and of future generations.

CONFLICT, RELIGION, PARADISE

Human Conflict and Neglect

Since the dawn of humanity's appearance on this planet, countless human beings have been killed, tortured, raped, or enslaved in the furtherance of one ideology or another. Countless innocents have been crushed and all hope extinguished in these violent orgies of death. The killing of a single human being, which should be unacceptable to modern humans, is a major tragedy. Violence should have no place in the affairs of modern humans.

History proves that the differences that separate us into many groups have been the source of human conflict, whether world wars based on political ideology, wars based on religious differences, "holy wars" driven by religious edicts, or smaller conflicts based on ethnic, tribal, or cultural differences. The single most infamous episode in the recent history of the human race in its immensity and abject cruelty must surely be the large-scale genocide perpetrated by Adolf Hitler and

his minions. The barbaric murder, torture, and elimi-
nation of eleven million innocent humans have rarely
been matched in all of human history. Yet did humans
learn profound lessons from World War II? In the 1992
to 1995 war in Bosnia-Herzegovina, Ratko Mladic, the
Serb commander, directed the killing of nearly eight
thousand innocent Muslim men and boys in Srebrenica.
As we step forth into this millennium, violent conflict is
pervasive. Instead of learning from history, the human
race seems determined to keep repeating it. Newfound
freedom in nations previously kept in bondage is often
replaced by sectarian wars and inhuman barbarism
that effectively crush the sweetness of freedom for its
citizens.

As the human race has progressed technologically, the
degree of violence that humans can inflict upon others has
increased exponentially as we developed powerful weap-
onry and new methods of mass destruction. The human
cost of Hitler's wars of occupation and genocide, the
merciless slaughter by the Axis powers, and the solution
deployed in Hiroshima and Nagasaki—the results of these
acts can be counted in the several millions of people killed,
injured, displaced, or left homeless. In modern times,
military weapons flooding into many nations have wound
up as instruments used by terrorist groups, militias, and
military or dictatorial regimes to brutalize, subjugate, and
enslave millions of innocents. Killings, rape, torture, ampu-
tations, and executions are widespread in some places. The
perpetrators of these crimes fear no system of justice, and

innocent millions suffer in silence with no hope of freedom. What drives humans to treat fellow humans with such callousness and cruelty?

I was born in a free India in 1953, six years after independence from British colonial rule. One chapter in India's history can serve as an important, painful example of how human conflict has tragic consequences. In the period leading up to independence, two leading Indian political parties existed: the Congress Party largely made up of Hindus, and the Muslim League. Their irreconcilable differences resulted in the plan to partition the country. Two nations, one Muslim and the other largely Hindu, were carved out of one. Millions of innocents were uprooted. Muslims who had for several centuries lived in Hindu areas were asked to migrate to Pakistan, and likewise Hindus from newly designated Pakistan were to migrate to India, a process that degenerated into horrific violence. The genesis of the violence is uncertain; however, the consequences were a monumental tragedy. Looting, murder, rape, and mayhem replaced the wishful plans of the leaders. With horrific violence breaking out against both groups, rumors and hysteria brought on innumerable orgies of death. The true stories of that time are almost unbelievable. Elders of both countries whose lives were touched by these events even today speak in hushed, bitter tones of the carnage and destruction. The sole vocal opponent of the partition was Mahatma Gandhi. However, he too had to acquiesce when he was told that it was partition or no freedom. With his profound wisdom, he felt that religious intolerance was no better than colonial rule, and the events that unfolded showed how prophetic his beliefs were. Yet the strong emotions that drowned reason at that time put both nations onto a disastrous course. Was this religion? Did it serve any religious need or purpose? Were the leaders of such violence given divine sanction to perpetrate the violence? What are the biological and human differences between Hindus and Muslims, or between any warring groups for that matter? Why are those who perpetrate horrific violence blind to their victims' humanity? What prevents the followers of a religion from recognizing the simple fact that we all belong to the same species?

Another example is Iraq after the fall of Saddam Hussein's regime, a tragedy of mindboggling proportions. Saddam Hussein and his sons, led one of the most brutal and cruel regimes in recent times. The populace of the country was brutalized and coerced into silence. The killing of innocents, mass murder with chemical agents, and other depredations are well documented. However, what followed after the Iraqis suddenly tasted freedom was a horrific human tragedy. Instead of coming together to rebuild a new nation, the wells of bitterness between the Shias and Sunnis poisoned the minds of violent elements, and the situation again degenerated into an orgy of death. The suicide bombings, torture, evisceration of living humans, enucleation of eyes, drilling of holes into the skulls of captives, raping of women, dousing of children with gasoline and burning them, and large-scale beheadings and executions were and are indefensible.

Religious and political ideologies that make humans blind to our oneness as a species result in the barbaric treatment of fellow humans that cannot be justified or accepted in this day and age.

In the last few decades, terrorism has become a central concern. The roots of terrorism, tragically, are based on love: love for one's religious or political group so strong and intense that one can be led to kill any perceived threats to that religion or political ideology. Terrorism comes from the denial of the humanity of others and the targeting of innocent humans as the "enemy." The leaders of such movements exhort young men and women to be the storm troopers of such wars. With widespread poverty and a lack of opportunity in failed states, it is no surprise that young men and women are not only willing to be recruited in such groups but are also willing to kill and become suicide bombers. In fact, these young humans are themselves victims of their own ideologies. The hopelessness of their existence makes them ripe targets for such causes. Followers of practically every major religion have resorted to terrorism in the past century. The real challenge is to show that absolute loyalty to a group should not blind one to the unity of all humans, who are all children of the same God or at least have a common origin.

Human conflict, then, is an immeasurable, tremendous tragedy. Yet today a far greater tragedy than human conflict exists: neglect. Nations' preoccupation with terrorism, violence, and defense against potential wars has led them to transfix their attention on conflict. While we spend enormous resources on wars or military preparedness against external threats, we are neglecting the most important issues of our time—issues that threaten our own very survival as a species.

The greatest challenge humans face at the dawn of our millennium is the need to resolve global armed conflict and instead direct precious resources and the boundless energy of humans toward the currently languishing major global issues. Apathy and listlessness are paths to failure. We have neglected threats to the very survival of all life forms so much that we now live in the most important century in the history of humans. What we do in this century will determine the long-term viability of this planet: supporting all forms of life or a slow but inevitable journey over the cliff of disaster. That being the seriousness of the consequence of neglect, can we afford to fail?

Religion in the Modern Age of Scientific Discovery

My religious development and search for the truth began at an early age. Born into a Protestant Christian family in India, I was groomed in the beliefs and practice of Christianity. At the age of nine I was admitted to a boarding school in the city of Bangalore. For nine months a year, I lived in a residential school far away from my family, a school full of boys drawn from all over India and from all the major faiths practiced in the country. The majority were Hindus. A small minority were Christians, both Catholic and Protestant. A few were Sikhs, and a small number were Muslims. We grew up together in complete harmony. We all spoke English and Hindi at school. Everyone spoke their mother tongue at home and represented all the languages spoken in India: Hindi, Punjabi, Tamil, Malayalam, Telugu, Kannada, Oriya, and so on. We developed friendships across these religious, cultural, and linguistic differences with no barriers at all. For three months a year, I was at home with my family during summer and winter holidays—a time to reconnect with my roots, attend church and Sunday school, and bask in the comfort of family. For nine months a year at school, no pressures or compulsions to attend church or even pray existed, so we took time for intellectual curiosity and a search for the truth.

All the boys in the school were similar in looks, build, and outlook, and yet my immediate family and grandparents were Christians. However, my ancestors had been Hindus. My forefathers had converted to Christianity because of

British missionaries. I was in a unique position to ask myself questions to which to this day I have never truly found the answers: Are Christians created by a Christian God and Hindus by Hindu gods? Are Muslims created by a separate God? When Hindus die, the soul goes through cycles of birth and reincarnation; when Christians die, their souls go to heaven or hell. When Hindus convert to Christianity, or the other way around, how do souls go to the right place? When Hindus convert to Christianity or Christians convert to Hinduism, do the gods become angry? What is the structure of our soul? Where are heaven and hell? Why can I see God only after I die? Why do all religions have a common belief—that only after death will we meet our maker? Why are there so many religions? Is there one true religion, and the others are false? How would I know which is the true religion? If the British had not come to India, I would likely be a Hindu. Would that have been the right religion? With so many religions and gods, do the gods of different religions talk with each other or fight with each other? If every person is created by the God of the religion he or she believes in, why do we all look alike?

I attended school, was a diligent student, and was happy in the pursuit of knowledge. Because I was free to explore different religious traditions I was excited and emboldened to ask such questions to understand what humans have pondered since the dawn of time: Who am I? Where am I? What am I? In a number of discussions with friends at school, family at home, and relatives who were Christian ministers, my search for the truth was an ongoing quest.

I truly enjoyed school, especially learning about science: botany, zoology, physics, chemistry, and astronomy. With true amazement we explored the complexity and true majesty of creation. As we learned about evolution and about the plant and animal kingdoms, I can still remember with absolute clarity the golden words of my biology teacher, Mr. Ramanujam: "Human beings are the highest form of mammals. We belong to the species *Homo sapiens.*" A bolt of lightning in my search for the truth, those words provided the flash of clarity that illuminated my search for God. On the one hand, there were a number of religions and gods, and on the other, we humans are just one species. The latter is a truth that was and is uncontroversial. The challenge is in reconciling our understanding of the truth and the different interpretations of different religions. We obviously have a common origin.

Why are there so many different religions and gods in different belief systems? I found the answer in another question: Why are there so many languages? My friends who hailed from different parts of India all had very different mother tongues. Over thousands of years, because of poor communication and the extremely slow pace of change, humans developed in discrete groups in isolation. Written language has existed only for the past five thousand years. Humans all over the world developed languages, each with different alphabets, grammar, vocabulary, and enunciation. In a country the size of India, twenty-three different languages developed—a testament to the versatility of the human brain. In a similar fashion, humans developed different religions, each with their own gods and god-desses, their own systems of beliefs, rituals, and rites. The names and imagery of gods differ, yet they share common-alities—for example, God as a creator whom we meet after our deaths. I said to myself, I am willing to follow the true religion if only one religion is true. Which religion should I follow? I prayed for enlightenment. However, I never had a vision to direct me in any particular direction. The silence left me confused, wondering why God did not speak to me. How do I know what to do?

In a world before television or Internet search engines, knowledge was freely available in the school library. Devouring books and encyclopedias, I developed a keen interest in astronomy, which provided perspective in my religious quest. Astronomy offers humans humility. It takes light one hundred thousand years to go across our own galaxy. Light travels at 186,000 miles per second! It takes light 13.798 billion years to reach us from the ends of the universe. And here I was a teenager trying to comprehend creation, God, religion, and life. I was at once struck by how transient and fleeting one human lifetime is and how very limited human knowledge is.

Humans have not yet set foot on another planet. We have no realistic way of travelling across our own galaxy, let alone the universe. Our ignorance of creation and this universe far exceeds our knowledge by a factor of several trillions. Hence human knowledge is far too limited in its scope for us to kill each other over these matters. If God were to appear to all humans at once and show us the way, it would make matters simple. Why does God not appear to all humans on a regular basis? No human can answer this question.

I graduated from high school with a great deal of interest in biology. I was admitted to a medical school and soon embarked on an amazing voyage of discovery. The first day of medical school started with a matter-of-fact entry into the world of human anatomy. As we nervously walked into the anatomy hall, we gazed at several tables with nude human corpses laid out in neat rows. When all clothes and coverings are cast aside, humans are so alike. While we bustled about dissecting different parts of the human body and studying the human skeleton, I asked myself the question: Was this human a Hindu, a Christian, or a Muslim? There was absolutely no way to tell. Muslim males are circumcised, but except for that, no one human being could be differentiated from another. In the histology laboratory, we studied different organ systems. I was amazed by the complexity and beauty of it all. Each and every part of the human body is a miracle. Would histology slides of different organs differ whether Hindu, Muslim, or a Christian? There was absolutely no difference. It became obvious to me during my preclinical studies that human beings are one. Mr. Ramanujam's words kept echoing in my mind: "Human beings are the highest form of mammals. We belong to the species *Homo sapiens.*"

My clinical training and years as a physician reinforced this truth repeatedly. My patients spoke various languages, believed in different religions, and were rich or poor; however, the presentation of disease, as well as its diagnosis and therapy, was identical for all of them. Except for a very few genetic diseases and inherited risk factors, that remains the truth. The oneness of human beings is uncontroversial in health and disease.

My patients have left me humbled and deeply honored. Without exception, their grace, courage, and gratitude have affected me profoundly. They are believers of all the major religions on earth, and yet I have not once encountered any challenges in being their doctor. I treat them and their religious beliefs with profound respect, and they in turn have never been concerned about my religious beliefs. We respect our common humanity and shared interrelated existence. As their doctor I have only found the best that humans possess.

In the forty years since I first entered medical school, I have been left in deep awe by the mountains of discoveries about the human body in health and disease. As scientific methods have increased in sophistication, the human body has been found to be amazingly complex—an absolute miracle. More complex and sophisticated than the vast majority of humans comprehend, our organ, cellular, and subcellular systems leave me speechless. The greatest human discovery of all time was decoding the human genome, which took tremendous human ingenuity to develop the tools and computing power to decipher it in a relatively short period of time. The human genome is such a gigantic and complex code of instruction that it leaves anyone with even an elementary understanding of it profoundly humbled. Francis Collins, the scientist who led the team of researchers that decoded the human genome, called it, "the language of God." His account of the efforts that led to this discovery is vividly detailed in his book titled *The Language of God*[1].

The human genome has profound lessons for all humankind. All major religions practiced today grew in the past five thousand years. Most religions have holy books written in the languages that humans have invented. The human genome is written in the language of God, in God's own alphabet, which evolved over hundreds of millions of years from the simplest life forms to present-day humans. Our DNA provides the code of instruction that controls the explosive growth that after the union of two cells results in a human. The early embryo divides into billions of cells that differentiate and migrate in a perfect manner to form a human with the most complex systems of any organism. Delve into the world of embryology, anatomy, histology, and physiology to study the miracle of life, and you will be left with a deep and profound respect for not only humans but all life forms. The greatest message that the human genome conveys is that all humans are one—a truth that cannot be brushed aside nor dismissed.

---

1 Francis Collins, *The Language of God* (New York: Simon & Schuster, 2006).

Our understanding and continued scientific discovery of the human genome will provide answers to how the human body truly functions, contributing to the understanding of diseases and their potential therapies. However, one genetic phenomenon is so amazing that it leaves me spellbound: human beings are believed to have evolved from a population of about sixty thousand humans living in Africa 160 thousand years ago. After migrating all across the globe, our numbers now stand at over seven billion. How many humans have ever lived on earth? Estimates are that 108 billion humans have ever been born on this planet.

So many of us, yet each one unique. The science of forensics has found that our fingerprints, palm prints, and foot prints are unique. The branching pattern of our retinal arteries is different. Our irises are unique. Subtle differences in face structures make each one of us unique. Every human has a unique and different voice, caused by subtle differences in the size and shape of the larynx, sinuses in the face, size and shape of the chest, and the centers in the brain that control speech. Each human's DNA is so unique that we now routinely and correctly incriminate criminals based on DNA evidence. It takes billions of cells to migrate in a well-ordered manner during embryonic growth to provide each of our unique identifiers. Let us model this mathematically: if a billion cells are involved in each person's unique identifiers, and 108 billion humans have existed, the genetic code in the two microscopic cells that combine to make a human being has such an enormously detailed instruction set that it can control the migration and growth of trillions of cells in 108 billion discrete humans. How this is accomplished is beyond human comprehension and one of nature's mysteries at which humans can only marvel. What is within the limits of human understanding is the persuasive truth that we are all interrelated, each surely part of one single species despite our genetic uniqueness.

The discovery of the human genome is so profound that it forces all humans to accept the humanity of others. No human being has the right to deny the humanity of another. If one believes in God as the creator, then all humans are created by the same God. Hence to kill another human being is to kill a human who has been created by the very same God. The challenge of our times is reconciling two facts: On one hand, we have more than twenty-one major religions and more than a billion humans who profess no religion. On the other, we have the human genome in God's own handwriting clearly showing us that all humans are one. Mere humans with our limited intellect cannot provide answers and explanations for the challenge of a multitude of religions. Every religious person must reflect upon the implications of the human genome written in God's own handwriting. To those who are atheists or agnostics and who do not believe in the existence of God or do not know if there is a God, the human genome has a profound message: the human genome is so complex and perfect that no matter what the origin of life is, human life and all life forms on earth are worthy of the most profound respect. We can differ in our beliefs about the origin of life and the existence of a creator; however, we are all confronted by a profound truth that human beings are one. We have a common origin and a common destiny. Hence even though we are human beings who believe in different religious faiths, we all belong to the species *Homo sapiens.*

There is no conflict between religion and science. Science provides the tools and methods to study the universe and all of creation. It gives us "eyes." In the interpretation of scientific discovery and religious beliefs a conflict seemingly exists. The real need is for human enlightenment. Human life, indeed all life on earth, is so complex, majestic, and beautiful that it without a doubt has a common origin. Respect for all humans must be the bedrock of all religions.

Any religion or political ideology that denies the humanity of any other human being is against the very nature of humanity and creation. In the past century, science has shown us this path of enlightenment. The path forward is simple: Truths that are written in the handwriting of God need to be viewed with the utmost respect. Respect for all humans has to be the basis of human existence. Respect for all religions and concern for the health and welfare of the followers of all religions is the only path to walk on.

The Planet Earth Is "Paradise" for the Species *Homo Sapiens*

The vision of human leaders has almost always been limited by the vision of the group from which they sprang forth. Some humans with narrow and shortsighted vision, whether they have led smaller groups or large nations, have failed to ask a fundamental question: Who speaks for the species *Homo sapiens*? Who speaks for all life forms on this planet? As *Homo sapiens* devours and decimates other life forms and destroys our planet's ecological systems and ability to sustain life as we know it, one truth arises, a truth so glaringly obvious I am amazed it has not produced consternation and alarm in every human mind: the planet Earth is "paradise" for the species *Homo sapiens* and for all life forms on this planet.

I mean no disrespect to any religion. Almost all religions believe in a paradise in the afterlife. However, in the lifetimes of all living creatures, the planet Earth is the only paradise we will know. A look toward the stars should teach us a few important facts. No planet or moon in our solar system can support the life forms that have evolved on this planet, whose basic requirements necessary for life which we take for granted probably do not exist in an identical manner elsewhere. If a planet identical to Earth does exist, where would we find it? To go across our own galaxy would take one hundred thousand light-years. Recorded human history by way of written language is only five thousand years old. Technologies to explore space have been invented in only the past hundred. Even if we were to develop technologies that could propel humans at the speed of light, can we even comprehend a journey that might take one hundred thousand years? Even a journey of one thousand years is beyond our comprehension when each human generation's useful adult lifespan lasts a mere fifty years. In realistic terms there is no other home for all of Earth's life forms. Larger ethical questions arise concerning colonizing other celestial bodies. We have, as a species, trashed this planet. The unplanned growth of humans and the polluting technologies we have developed have ravaged this paradise. Are we responsible enough to settle colonies anywhere outside this planet, without polluting and destroying pristine planets, moons, or any other bodies that may come within our grasp? Should we not put our house in order before we leap for the stars?

Religious, national, political, linguistic, and ethnic issues have long held the center stage of human affairs. Industrialization and modern technologies have been a blessing in so many ways and yet a curse on the long-term survival of all life forms on this planet. Given that no other home for all of Earth's life forms exists, the destruction of this planet's life-sustaining systems is the biggest crime *Homo sapiens* has committed, one for which our species must take responsibility.

Who speaks for the species *Homo sapiens*? We have reached a critical juncture in the history of this living planet. The leaders of humanity must seek enlightenment and speak with one voice: we come from different lands, we believe in different religions, we speak different languages, and yet we are all *Homo sapiens*. It is the duty of every human to protect and preserve this planet. It is time for all humans to be unified in one of the most important peaceful revolutions in history—the revolution to save the planet.

If the planet Earth cannot support human life, we will have no religions, nations, languages, or ethnic groups. Our needs as a species transcend the needs of each subgroup. Leaders should exhort the followers of every religion, nation, or ethnic group to consider measures to preserve and nurture this planet. The global effort to save the planet and to reestablish the planet as a paradise for all life forms for millions of years into the future is our most important duty and responsibility. Our entire existence on this planet must evolve from this fundamental obligation. Religion, nationhood, and the myriad ways we divide ourselves must be woven into the primary obligation of human existence: preserving and nurturing this paradise. This lofty goal will not be actualized by wishful thinking. This lofty goal will not be realized by dreaming and talking endlessly about it. This lofty goal will be achieved by having crystal-clear plans to move *Homo sapiens* from its destructive, fragmented, and violent current practices to a state of peaceful and productive coexistence. That is the legacy we must leave behind for our children and for countless generations to come. As the highest life form on this planet, we have an obligation to each other and to every form of life on this planet. We truly are the custodians of this planet.

As a mere physician, I cannot even begin to understand the enormity and complexity of the tasks needed to achieve this goal. The plans outlined in the rest of this book may be considered unrealistic or even naïve. However, this book is truly a call to action. We must build a coalition of nations and open our arms to include all nations that will join in this endeavor. It is time to harness modern technologies for the most valuable role they can play: to rebuild the planet and preserve it as a paradise for all life forms that have evolved. I am certain that in a short period of time the interests of the entire species can be aligned, and we can walk into the future on a path we have never dreamed to walk on, together as one people with a common purpose.

THE PATH TO AN ENLIGHTENED EXISTENCE

An Anthem for a Free World

In a monumental tragedy, as human beings in many places are crushed by violent regimes, hope is being replaced by immense and abject fear. We are the highest form of mammals and yet the most brutal. Animals in the jungle kill for food or survival. There is no instance where large groups of animals are enslaved by a ruling regime with no hope for freedom. Human history is replete with forms of slavery, colonization, and the subjugation of men, women, and children. Learning about vicious regimes that rape and torture humans leaves one with a heavy heart and full of sorrow about what humans are capable of. Freedom is the birthright of every human. There can be no progress toward the goals that we need to accomplish unless the winds of freedom caress every human heart. Despite the violent suppression of freedom and the systematic rape and brutalization of women in failed states across the world, the deep yearning for freedom and hope for a bright future for the world's children can never be extinguished.

When India shuddered under British colonial rule, Rabindranath Tagore, the Nobel Prize-winning poet from India, put into eloquent words in 1913 an anthem that resonated in every Indian heart. A century later, millions of humans are in a far worse predicament. An anthem that every nation must aspire to, it is an ideal that every man, woman, and child must claim as their birthright.

Where the Mind Is without Fear

Where the mind is without fear and the head is held high
Where knowledge is free
Where the world has not been broken up into fragments by narrow domestic walls
Where words come out from the depth of truth
Where tireless striving stretches its arms towards perfection
Where the clear stream of reason has not lost its way into the dreary desert sand of dead habit
Where the mind is led forward by thee into ever-widening thought and action
Into that heaven of freedom, my Father, let my country awake

—Rabindranath Tagore, 1913

This beautiful poem is truly an anthem for a free world. To citizens of nations who are suppressed by violent regimes, to women who are brutalized and enslaved, and to all humans whose freedoms have been snatched away, this anthem will surely resonate in their hearts. The species *Homo sapiens* will never realize its rightful place on this planet until all its members are free.

Any nation that suppresses its people, any nation that does not treat its women with respect and as equal citizens, will not last. No force can permanently suppress the hope and yearning for freedom. Freedom is life itself. It will always spring forth and bloom. This is a basic law of nature. In this modern age of instant and open communication, suppression of individual freedoms and brutal acts of violence are witnessed by billions in a matter of seconds. For nations that have effectively enslaved their people, the writing on the wall is clear: Freedom for your citizens is inevitable. Take the initiative for a peaceful transition to freedom, prosperity and happiness. This is their birthright.

We must harness the boundless energy of every man and woman if we are to restore this planet to a state where it is truly a paradise for humans and all forms of life. The pace at which our only planet is being degraded does not give us the luxury of time; only free citizens of freedom-loving countries can hope to work toward rebuilding it. Totalitarian regimes serve their own self-interest. The best interests and needs of their own people have been trivialized. Hence they are largely unconcerned about the major issues that humans face today. Rebuilding and preserving this planet is inextricably linked to freedom and world peace, goals which are inseparably intertwined. Idealism and hope must drive plans, and this is only possible with countries whose citizens are free.

How do we reach out to citizens of failed states brutalized by violent regimes and move them onto the road to freedom, prosperity, and peace? How to transform this mighty force into one that works to reestablish this planet as a true paradise? How do we design practical plans to achieve this? A comprehensive plan that is clear in its goals and encompasses all the facets of this complex challenge is something we need to address with a sense of immense urgency.

We need to move toward a world free of fear—where there is no fear of hunger, poverty, disease, or homelessness; where there is no fear for one's safety, liberty, and freedom. A world without fear should be a fundamental goal—a world where every human can hold his or her head high, a world where humans tirelessly strive to protect and nurture the only home that we know. That is the true path ahead for the species *Homo sapiens* today.

A World Federation of Democracies:
The Only Path to a Free, Peaceful, and Prosperous World

Human beings have been subjected to many different forms of government in which their freedoms have been suppressed: from being serfs in the service of royalty to being brutally subjugated by dictators and theocratic regimes. In all this, one simple fact has often been brushed aside: Every human voice is to be cherished in a nation. Every human voice is to be heard in a nation. Every issue of governance requires popular support. As we head out into this millennium, we must recognize this universal truth. The only form of governance that respects every human voice is a free democracy. A democratic form of governance is the only model truly worthy of human beings.

Citizens, both men and women, of free democratic countries go about their lives with no fear of a ruling apparatus. Citizens of nations that groan under the tyranny of brutal regimes strain against the chains that enslave them and constantly yearn to break free from a life of fear. They yearn to enjoy the liberties that are their birthright. The inhuman killings and systematic torture and rape of women, men, and children that are used as strategies to strike fear in people's hearts are an abomination that must be brought to an immediate end. Unfortunately, no single nation has the might and resources to stamp out such depraved acts in other nations. While the United Nations has often intervened, responding to genocide and torture on a large scale, its actions have often been far too late.

Several lessons arose from World War II. Adolf Hitler was perhaps the most depraved human in the long history of humanity. With megalomaniacal ambitions of global domination, he not only launched military campaigns to achieve this end but also systematically killed eleven million innocent men, women, and children in the concentration camps of Auschwitz, Dachau, and the other factories of death. The entry of America into this global conflict turned the tide. As free nations united themselves in the Allied effort, they managed to get onto the road to victory and freedom for the entire world. It is a tragedy of our times that the sacrifices of the Allied forces of World War II have been forgotten by the world. What would have happened if America had not been drawn into the conflict or lacked the political courage, leadership, and foresight to battle Hitler and the Axis powers? What would have happened if the Allied forces had not formed an alliance? Adolf Hitler would have defeated the other nations in Europe and rolled over Africa, Asia, Russia, and China. He would then have isolated America and likely defeated it. If Hitler's plans had succeeded, the Nazi flag would be fluttering today over every city and country. The killing of eleven million humans would have been a tea party compared to the horrors the world would have seen. Hundreds of millions would have been exterminated or enslaved based on Hitler's world vision of who was unfit to live. There would have been no Christianity, Islam, Hinduism, or any form of religion other than Aryan nationalism. The Vatican, Mecca, Jerusalem, Benares, and all other holy places would have been destroyed and eliminated. The entire planet would have become Hitler's godless empire. To all those who rail against America or all the nations who were part of the Allied forces in World War II, I can only humbly say that the world owes a debt of gratitude to all those who laid down their lives, were injured, or fought as part of a global effort to destroy the ambitions of the leaders of the Axis powers. We are free because of those brave men and women. Let us not have any misconceptions about their sacrifice. We are free because of them.

During World War II, my father was a soldier in the Indian army under command of the British. He fought in Italy, the Middle East, and the Far East. The number of officers and enlisted men in the Indian army who died in World War II is estimated to be about thirty six thousand despite India not being one of the major nations in that war. This was a tremendous sacrifice in the global effort to secure a free world. The Indian officers and soldiers who fought alongside the rest of the Allies were Hindus, Muslims, and Christians drawn from every corner of India. The Allied effort was truly a mighty alliance with the common purpose of fighting against world domination. Estimates of the total number of humans killed, including civilians, range from fifty to seventy million. As I remember my late father's stories of his war experience, I am humbled by the enormity of the sacrifices of his generation.

It is time for nations all across the world to remember, honor, and forever be grateful for the millions who perished fighting for a free world in the Second World War.

Every religion and nation, without exception, has survived that dark period in the history of humanity only because of them. World War II taught us that when the leadership and the ruling apparatuses of a country are abjectly cruel, innocent citizens are trapped in a regime where any dissension is met with imprisonment and torture or death. Leaders of such nations have armies of soldiers and officers who are obligated to follow orders or be executed. Once such leadership and ruling apparatuses are eliminated and their war machines dismantled, peace and freedom permit the innocent citizens and subsequent generations to wash away the memories and depraved ambitions. Citizens of Germany, Japan, and Italy today, who have grown up in free and democratic societies, are as fine humans as citizens of any country in the collection of democratic nations. While their parents or grandparents were forced to fight wars that were not of their choice, today's citizens of these countries overwhelmingly vote for peace. Today, the enemies of the Allied nations of World War II are democratic nations allied with us.

NATO (the North Atlantic Treaty Organization) serves as an important example of a strategy to wean humans away from conflict toward a productive, peaceful existence. NATO came into being in 1949. It was a system of collective defense whereby member states agreed to mutual defense in response to an attack by any external party. It is probably the most important reason that we have not had a global war since the Second World War. The combined military might of this alliance of democratic nations has been the greatest deterrence to large-scale wars. It led to the fall of communism and the clear ascension of democracy in the last sixty years.

Hence the best strategy to bring nations away from conflict and strife is to develop a large global alliance of democratic nations. This must be a political, military, and economic alliance of free nations wedded to democracy—a federation of nations that supports all religions and cultures and asks its citizens to lay down arms and walk on the path of peace. None of the member states would permit terrorist groups to operate within their borders. Any external armed threat to any nation in the alliance would be a threat to the whole alliance. Federation forces would respond to such threats. Any internal armed threat to the democratically elected government would be a threat to the federation, inviting a response. Citizens of the member states of this federation would have the basic freedoms enjoyed in any democratic nation, including freedom of speech and religion. Nations that join the federation would be given financial support and preferential status for investment and trade by developed countries.

While the United States, Britain, France, Italy, Germany, Australia, and Canada have been the champions of democracy, this global alliance would include Russia, India, Japan, Pakistan, South Korea, and every other democratic nation. As newly formed democracies are born, they are extremely fragile and vulnerable. Having the automatic military support of the super and regional powers would prevent any backsliding. As young democratic nations join the alliance and reap its benefits, they would serve as examples for other nations to join the federation. I am confident that the free citizens of the world would come together to live in peace and work together toward a bright future for themselves, their children, and for generations to come.

Is world peace contingent on abolishing nuclear weapons? Abolishing nuclear weapons today would not make this a safer planet at this time in human history. Human beings had been at war for thousands of years before the development of nuclear weapons. Both World War I and World War II began before nuclear weapons were developed. Hence if we were to hypothetically destroy all nuclear weapons and all capabilities and knowledge of making nuclear weapons, would the world be a safer place? The answer is a resounding no. A large number of local and regional conflicts would break out as nations would have no fear of being stopped. If only conventional wars were possible and fear of major powers intervening in large-scale conflict were slim, wars would erupt in several parts of the world. The key is for all the states with nuclear weapons capabilities to combine their might in a single federation of democracies. By combining their strengths in a democratic alliance, they minimize or eliminate the risk of nuclear war. I do see, in the distant future, human beings and nations becoming enlightened enough to dismantle nuclear weapons and the armies of the world—an age when humans would consider the killing of a single human being an abominable crime. Nuclear weapons are not killing any human beings today.

The greatest concern today is the acquisition of nuclear weapons by states with no respect for human life or those that have the stated mission of destroying other nations. Concern for nuclear weapons being used to destroy millions of innocent humans is real, and the prevention of the acquisition of nuclear weapons technologies by such states has to be the most important strategy today.

This brings us to the question of China, a communist nation and a nuclear power. China's communist leadership is immensely proud of its achievements and the amazing growth of its economy. China's economic success is indeed impressive. However, China is yet another example of the success of democracies around the world. China's booming economy is largely due to the massive influx of investments and technologies from the developed democracies of the world. The cheap labor in China has led to the gigantic export of products to rich countries around the world. The influx of technologies has led to the modernization of its own manufacturing capabilities. Hence in a very real sense, communism has failed in China. The prosperity it sees is a toast to democracies and the free countries of the world. The tragedy in China is that Chinese workers labor tirelessly to produce goods for countries where personal freedoms are a birthright. Yet these same workers do not enjoy these simple freedoms in their own land. China is home to brilliant minds, amazing intellectuals, and an industrious and peace-loving populace. As young Chinese discover the world and watch the freedoms that citizens of democracies enjoy, the writing on the wall is very clear: China will become a free democratic nation. It is merely a matter of time. China deserves a democracy as much as any other nation in the world.

The economic success of any nation depends on internal peace and stability, the absence of armed conflict with its neighbors, the education of youth, and the hard work and enterprise of its citizens. This is the only path to prosperity for nations. A World Federation of Democracies could usher in peace and stability to help tackle urgent global problems. It is time to move away from conflict and focus the world's attention and might on the huge global problems that urgently need to be addressed. This is a time when we need a mighty alliance of nations to usher in a golden age, where we work shoulder to shoulder to save the planet from the disastrous consequences of human folly.

Millennium of the Girl Child

What should the role of women be in societies? As we look at nations around the world, the current status of women varies from leading nations and having equal opportunities with men to being enslaved by men and treated no better than cattle. As societies and cultures have evolved over the past several millennia, we have moved far away from our biological moorings.

I have had the privilege of watching nature's creatures around our home in Minnesota, in the United States of America. On a nearby lake, I often notice the Canada geese, which offer humans an important lesson. During spring the geese fly up from warm southern states, and small flocks of these geese call this lake their home. Within a few weeks of their annual migration to this lake, a number of goslings are hatched. The adults and "children" swim on the lake, busy feeding and exploring. It is delightful on some days to see most of the adults fly off to explore the surrounding areas while the entire brood of twelve to fifteen goslings is taken care of by two of the geese. By the evening, the rest of the adults fly back to this large community—such is their amazing sense of family and community. As spring turns into summer, the goslings begin to look like their parents. They gain in strength and learn to fly. As the first flakes of snow fall, the entire flock is ready to fly south, to winter in the warm southern states. Males and females must fly thousands of miles to escape the harsh Minnesota winters. Males and females fly as equal partners. Nature did not create females of this species so weak that they cannot fly like the males. If the females were frail and unable to fly, the entire species would be wiped out in one northern winter. The lesson that humans must draw from this humble species is amazingly clear: Women and men must be equal partners if the species *Homo sapiens* is to thrive.

The education of children, both male and female, has to be the foundation for any nation. Equal opportunities for men and women to be employed in gainful, productive occupations are the building blocks of modern society. Since human beings appeared on this planet, women have been vulnerable as they conceived and gave birth to children. Before modern contraception when repeated pregnancies were the norm, the responsibility of raising children was women's primary roles. With the advent of widespread education and the availability of modern methods of contraception, families have become smaller. Women have taken to practically all the occupations in which men alone were previously employed. Educating women empowers them to take better care of their own health and that of their families: child immunization rates rise dramatically, family sizes are limited, and both infant and maternal mortality rates drop. The key to limiting the global population explosion and improving the health of human societies is the education of women. This simple fact has been emphasized by experts for decades.

In a few religious societies and cultural groups, the education of women is condemned, and men forcibly shut down schools for girls and prevent them from studying. In many instances such denial is brutally enforced, truly reflecting a lack of enlightenment about changes in modern human life. When women are uneducated, segregated, and confined to their families or to women-only activities, who takes care of their health care needs? Consider pregnancy. Modern medicine has completely changed the equation of life and death. Prenatal care requires educated, well-trained doctors and midwives to monitor the pregnancy; pelvic examinations are needed to choose between natural childbirth and cesarean sections; ultrasound examinations are routinely performed to monitor the growth of the child. Difficulties in labor may require an emergency cesarean section. Vaginal examinations, Pap smears, breast examinations, mammograms, routine colonoscopies, and other preventative procedures are routine in modern medicine. If women are ignorant and illiterate, this role must be performed by men unless such societies outlaw modern health care for women. Should women not be treated for medical and surgical emergencies? Should a woman have to be covered from head to foot outside her home and yet have medical examinations and procedures performed by male doctors?

A thousand years ago, almost all adult men and women were illiterate. Most worked on farms, shepherded cattle, or had other simple occupations. The written word was confined to a small segment of most societies. Health care was nonexistent, and other women helped conduct deliveries. Education and industrialization have brought dramatic change in the past few centuries. Modern occupations demand education and advanced training. In medicine, the advances are so great that practices in medieval times deserve no comparison. Today, keeping women in bondage is detrimental to men and society as a whole. Societies that do not believe in the education of women suffer the consequences of high infant and maternal mortality rates and poor health among the whole population. Is it not time for religious and political leaders to take the lead in changing the expectations for women in their societies? Societies that systematically enslave women are destined to fail.

The systematic rape of women as a strategy in war is horrific and painful. The perpetrators of such heinous acts fail to understand: There is no honor in raping a defenseless woman, man, or child. There is no honor in torturing, maiming, or killing a defenseless human being. In failed societies we find primitive health care, nonexistent economies and fragile social systems unable to cope with disease, famine, or floods. Hence the repercussions of a failed society are reaped by the rapists and torturers themselves. AK-47 automatic rifles and military weapons do not cure diarrhea, dysentery, cholera, or tuberculosis. AK-47s do not immunize children against polio, measles, mumps, rubella, or whooping cough. AK-47s do not improve infant and maternal mortality rates. A failed society ultimately kills the families of the violent actors and those actors themselves. A nation immersed in horrific internal violence is dying a slow death.

The message to parents who care about their children is simple: hold your sons and daughters close to your hearts, listen to their dreams, and try to help them fulfill them. By doing so, you determine your own happiness and the happiness and prosperity of your families, communities, societies, and nations. Boys have been given the pride of place for many millennia; today it is time to support boys and girls as equals. If your daughter wants to be a teacher, nurse, doctor, lawyer, engineer, or the president of your nation, then it is your duty as a parent to help her achieve her dreams. In her happiness lies your own happiness.

The role of the modern woman in society is not inconsistent with the real values of any religion or society. For example, Minnesota has a large and vibrant community of immigrants from Somalia, some of them families who have fled the horrific violence in their own lands and now call America their home. I have several patients from this community, and it is a privilege to take care of their cardiac medical needs. With a great sense of pride I watch members of this community embrace life in America while still following their own cultural traditions. I have watched with great pride as Somali women in their traditional hijab move freely around the city. They drive cars, take their children to doctor's appointments, or go shopping by themselves. I see groups of Somali women in malls laughing, so happy to be free. They have no fear of being molested or raped. Somalis here need not fear being caught up in horrific violence. They worship freely in mosques and vote in elections. Boys and girls attend school. I have met a number of young women who work as translators for adults who speak little English. These young, bright women have a glow on their faces as they proudly recount to me their continuing education efforts and ambitions to become doctors, nurses, or pharmacists. The women and men of this wonderful community are as fine Muslims as anyone in any country on this planet—devout, decent, and great humans. As nations across the world grapple with the role of women in societies and their freedoms, I think that the women of the Somali community in Minnesota make excellent role models. We see the greatness of the United States when the religious and personal freedoms of this minority Muslim community are fully protected by a nation of predominantly Christians.

Nations where women and men are educated and have equal opportunities will continue to be the most developed in the world. No nation can hope to move the wheels of progress unless every able man and woman puts his or her shoulders to the task of going forward. As we start this millennium, that truth is self-evident, but we need enlightened leaders. No nation, religion, society, or community should stand in the way of the rightful place of women in modern times. As citizens of nations around the world strain at freeing themselves from autocratic societies, women need to assert themselves and define for themselves their roles in such evolving societies. We do not exist in a medieval world. Societies and nations will evolve and prosper in direct proportion to the education and equality of women in such societies.

We truly live in the millennium of the girl child. While the world has always supported and educated its sons, it is time for us to treat sons and daughters as equals. It is time to firmly place the future of this planet in the capable hands of our young men and women so that we may succeed.

ACHIEVING CRITICAL GOALS

Global Plans for a Thousand Years, One Century at a Time

As *Homo sapiens* goes about its destructive ways, ravaging life-sustaining systems on this planet, it is not always obvious within our short span of life where we are headed and what needs to be done to stop and then reverse the course. Scientists from many disciplines have been sounding the warning bells for decades. However, their cries seem to fall on the deaf ears of those in a position to make a difference. An enlightened position is to foresee and plan for a future that extends far beyond one's own lifetime. Most humans can influence the course of events in their own lives from about age eighteen to age seventy or so (with some exceptions at both ends of the spectrum). Fifty years is a very short span of time on this planet, and yet, considering the speed at which this planet's life-sustaining ability is being destroyed, even the next fifty years could be catastrophic at the rate at which this carnage is unfolding. To truly understand the magnitude of the folly of our species, we need to view the consequences a millennium from today and plan for them one century at a time. We need to carry plans from generation to generation into the distant future to achieve a vision of the highest form of creatures on earth living at peace with themselves as wise custodians of all life forms and natural resources on this planet.

Planning for eternity is neither novel nor unprecedented. Worldwide, most royal kingdoms in history passed on power to the heirs to the throne from generation to generation. Royal families planned to rule until the end of time. Modern humans plan for their deaths with wills specifying distribution of their estates and worldly possessions. The pharaohs of ancient Egypt built the pyramids to stand for eternity. Even today, almost five thousand years later, these works stand in their majesty, awing modern humans. Five thousand years from today this planet will no longer be able to support the burgeoning human masses if we continue to hurtle along the current path of assured destruction. Future generations will only agonize over the folly of humans who lived in this century and launched this planet over the precipice.

The next hundred years, and especially the next fifty, are the most critical in bringing to a screeching halt the multipronged destruction of life-sustaining ecosystems and the decimation of other species. The time to act is now. Saving civilization should transcend forms of government, language, culture, and race. The call today is for all nations across the world to come together to stop the ruinous course we have taken and help nurture this planet, making it a beautiful home for all life forms for millions of years into the future.

We need clear plans for how to get there, executed by all nations to finally achieve what we should already have today: a paradise for all life forms living in harmony and in balance with nature.

The United Nations' Millennium Development Goals, developed as a collaborative effort among numerous nations, are a beacon of hope asserting that cooperative focus on solving urgent global problems should be a top priority. The laudable goals of the program are:

1) Eradicate extreme poverty and hunger
2) Achieve universal primary education
3) Promote gender equality and empower women
4) Reduce child mortality
5) Improve maternal health
6) Combat HIV/AIDS, malaria, and other diseases
7) Ensure environmental sustainability
8) Develop a global partnership for development.

This multifaceted program has not received the global support, visibility, and funding it needs to achieve most of its goals and, going forward, to set far more aggressive goals. Development is once again being sidelined by conflict.

A mere cardiologist is not skilled in any of the areas where we need to strive or in the planning or execution of such global plans. The following sections must be viewed as a crude sketch of a "big picture." It is merely an outline of some of the critical elements from the viewpoint of a nonexpert. These are suggested components of a plan with well-defined goals. With universal support and consensus, we can achieve these goals, even if only well after our own lifetimes. This is a call to action. We must rise to meet the challenge or let the planet perish as a home for all living creatures.

THE NEXT ONE HUNDRED YEARS: CRITICAL ELEMENTS OF A COMPREHENSIVE GLOBAL PLAN

Zero Population Growth by the Year 2030

The majority of population growth forecasts go only up to the year 2050. We probably cannot accurately forecast what the population of humans would be in the year 3014. Some indicators show the population explosion slowing. UN predictions are that it will stabilize at 9.22 billion in 2075 and decline to 8.97 billion by 2300[2].Surely, it does not even matter what the actual number may hypothetically be. The seven billion humans currently on earth are already far too many for this planet. Scientists have calculated that we need the natural resources of one and a half Earths to sustain even the present population! When did the population "explode"? Let us look at two simple

---

2 *World Population to 2300*.United Nations Publications, New York 2004.

pieces of information. World population is estimated to have been 310 million in the year 1000 AD. The trajectory of population growth since then is astounding, reaching one billion in 1804 and today surpassing seven billion. If we look just at the years since modern methods of contraception became available, since around 1950, the population has increased from two and a half billion to more than seven billion today.

The uncontrolled population explosion of the species *Homo sapiens* is the basic driver and multiplier of all other issues. Modern medicine's ability to prevent early and premature deaths from diseases that decimated human populations in the past, coupled with explosive birthrates, has produced unplanned exponential growth—the greatest human folly. Some describe *Homo sapiens* as a cancer on this planet. A cancer is characterized by the uncontrolled growth of a group of cells that invades surrounding structures, has a high metabolic rate, and can finally result in the death of the patient. However, there is a vast difference between cancers and humans, the most important being that as humans we have the means to stop this uncontrolled population explosion by ourselves. Tragically, we do not have the collective wisdom or the will to limit our population to what this planet can sustain, and instead we have stripped vast areas of forests for farming, for fuel, for construction materials, and for the inexorable expansion of cities and villages. We have decimated hundreds of species of animals and, in search of food and using modern technologies we have depleted the oceans of marine life and destroyed the coral forests that sustain it. As our population and its needs exponentially increase, we have no other natural resources to sustain this unnatural growth. Hence *Homo sapiens*, the highest form of mammals, is slowly but surely devouring the very life-sustaining systems it needs to survive.

There must be a balance among the number of humans and life-sustaining systems on this planet and all other life forms. We have tilted the balance to our own detriment. This cancerous growth of humans can be stopped—by humans. We have the power to do that. Why have we not already done that? Are we not completely irresponsible as a species?

I have often wondered how many human beings could be housed on this planet, living in balance with nature, with all our current polluting modern technologies? I would suggest that the optimal number is probably around two hundred million. Seven billion is already far too many. Overpopulation is the central problem we face today. Yet no significant movement or program seeks to achieve a zero population growth rate. Instead we have a complete paralysis of thought and action in dealing with this monumental folly.

Nations around the world are transfixed with multiple issues related to conflict. The world's attention is focused on greenhouse gases and their deleterious effects. A great deal of research, debate, and concern revolves around limiting CO_2 emissions and finding alternate sources of energy. These are important issues; however, the multiplier is the human population explosion. Yet there is practically no public debate about this issue. No global program—absolutely no visible global effort—conveys the urgency and overriding importance of achieving this goal. A comprehensive program to achieve a zero population growth rate is of prime importance. The complete lack of support for and denial of the importance of this issue, worldwide, is completely unacceptable.

I also wonder where we would be today if the leaders of the twentieth century had had the vision and wisdom to come together and work toward goals that would have benefited all of humankind. Could the global human population have been frozen at two billion or less? Could nonpolluting sources of energy have been developed to be the major sources of energy today? All our problems would have been of a far lower magnitude.

Can we achieve a zero population growth rate by the year 2030? The model we need to study is the success of the World Health Organization (WHO) in eradicating smallpox. Smallpox was a scourge which has now been eradicated from this planet. With a high mortality rate and severe facial disfigurement, smallpox had been present for all of recorded human history. The benefits of eradicating the disease were obvious to all nations. The WHO, with the support of nations all over the world, launched a global immunization program that finally eradicated the disease in the 1970s. The consequences of the population explosion that continues unabated are far graver than that of a single disease. The need to stop this growth is far more important for the well-being of this planet than leaders around the world comprehend. It is time to launch a global program with the clear objective of achieving a zero population growth rate on a war footing.

A large number of experts in the WHO and governmental and nongovernmental agencies worldwide, given the resources and a clear goal, can develop ZPG programs. Obviously, a first step is to make birth control and contraception free and universally available, along with a massive global health education campaign. There need to be tangible financial incentives for the adoption of permanent methods of birth control. The education of women has to be an integral part of the program. World leaders have never articulated this issue as being important. Enlightened leadership should bring the ZPG goal onto the world stage as the most important program of the next decade. Global funds can be easily made available by nations across the world if we have the political will. We can achieve a zero population growth rate by the year 2030 if we make it our first and most important goal.

Synthetic or Synthesized Foods?

We have already effectively outgrown the capacity of natural methods of farming, raising livestock, or fishing for food. This planet was never designed to hold or feed so many humans. If a ship were to set sail on a long voyage, an essential part of the plans would be to provision adequate food and drink. On modern airline flights, this concept is of no concern to most of us; however, if we were to embark on a space flight to Mars that might take six months each way, a critical part of the planning would be the provisioning of food and water. The planet Earth is the ultimate spaceship. It provides for all living creatures. We have already far exceeded its capacity to support us. Where do we go from here?

Human beings, with their amazing intelligence, have invented efficient methods of farming, raising livestock, and harvesting fish from lakes, rivers, and oceans. However, fundamentally we are as dependent on natural sources of food as the earliest humans. The conventional vision of better farming methods, high-yield seeds, better fertilizers, and weed killers can increase the yield per acre of land, but human needs will outstrip the capacity of even the most optimistic projections of increasing food production. Unregulated fishing has led to dwindling fish stocks, and in the foreseeable future, the oceans will cease to be a source of significant amounts of food.

We need to develop the ability to synthesize basic nutritional components on an industrial scale in gigantic "green" factories. Proteins, fats, and carbohydrates are the essential components of all forms of food. Our methods of sourcing food need to undergo a seismic shift if we want to feed the billions of humans on this planet. We must bring in brilliant minds and fund the research and development of methods of synthesizing nutritional components on an industrial scale. There is already work done in this field, so mine is definitely not an original suggestion. If we could put men on the moon, decode the human genome, and develop modern methods of travel, we should be able to achieve this goal, too. We need to support nascent discoveries in this field, fund new research, and scale up production rapidly.

At least 75 percent of human nutritional needs must be synthesized in factories with a zero carbon footprint. We should aim to achieve this goal by the year 2050—a giant step to contemplate. If we achieve this goal, we will have solved one of the greatest challenges we face today: feeding more humans than this planet can sustain. It would also be the most important step in stopping the degradation of this planet. With funding from nations across the world, in a collaborative effort, and bringing in brilliant minds to work on this problem, nutritional security can be achieved. I would foresee such technologies as open to all humans: factories owned by governments of nations across the world manufacturing food to feed billions. We then could move away from destructive farming practices and dependence on the weather to a stable, assured source of food for all people. The greatest tragedy would be for such technologies to be protected by patents to provide an incentive for profit given that this strategy would fulfill a fundamental need and needs to be owned by all of humankind. What would it cost to fund global research with realistic expectations of success in this field? I would hazard an estimate of two hundred billion dollars to jumpstart massive research in this field.

Producing synthetic food is one of the most important global issues facing us today. The technical issues are solvable, whether it is the actual synthesis of proteins, fats, and carbohydrates or massive methods of cell culture to grow food components. Can we achieve in factories what nature does in agricultural fields, livestock farms, or in the oceans? When I joined a medical school in 1970, the first coronary artery bypass surgery had not been performed, and methods of percutaneous coronary interventions were not even conceptualized. Today these are routine procedures all over the globe. Once it was believed that operating on the human heart was foolish and uniformly fatal. Today the human heart is stopped, with patients connected to heart-lung machines, diseased valves replaced with artificial prosthetic valves, arteries bypassed, or damaged hearts transplanted with excellent success. The limitations are really in our minds. Synthetic foods, solving the biggest challenge of feeding billions around the globe, will be widely consumed and become a staple of the human diet. We need a global program that receives the attention, visibility, and support it deserves.

Ninety Percent of Global Energy Needs from Green Sources by the Year 2050

The large global debate surrounding green energy sources has led to substantial effort put forth in developing them. We have invested billions of dollars in the research and development of technologies that could potentially revolutionize where we get our energy. As a physician I can provide absolutely no technical insight. Still, I would like to offer one perspective: our preoccupation with issues of conflict and religious and political ideological differences has plainly hijacked the enormous resources that should be used in moving this field forward. The fundamental issue that prevents progress in the field is not the lack of technologies but our failure to adopt them. We can generate the immense amount of power that humans consume, but we must reduce our needs for such power and adopt existing green sources of energy generation.

We need to develop a global consensus to gradually switch to green sources of energy. A technological miracle might perhaps provide solutions, but for now we need to wean ourselves off coal, gasoline, nuclear power, and natural gas for energy production and switch to nonpolluting sources. The switch to solar, wind, and tidal power generation on a massive scale is the first step. We may never be able to completely eliminate the use of fossil fuels; however, the change to green sources will come only from global adoption. The rate of CO_2 production by humans is horrific. We are poisoning and, slowly but surely, killing the planet.

One single nation showing the world that it can meet 90 percent of its energy needs from green sources would be the turning point. I am certain that this can be done in a short timeframe.

Perfect Waste Management by 2050

Homo sapiens, the highest form of mammals, has distinguished itself from all other life forms by generating monumental amounts of garbage and refuse and, more important, waste products that do not decompose or biodegrade—one of the tragedies of the human population explosion and a direct consequence of modern technologies. According to the World Bank document "What a Waste: A Global Review of Solid Waste Management (2012)," 1.3 billion tons of municipal solid waste (MSW) are produced every year as a result of the modern urban lifestyle. This excludes nonurban waste. By 2025 it is anticipated that MSW will grow to 2.2 billion tons per year. We are far from disposing of these mountains of garbage appropriately. Recycling programs are inadequate and often nonexistent in many countries. Hence we have a huge problem—we're trashing this beautiful planet. Every nation is responsible for this unacceptable and delinquent behavior.

Human brilliance led to the development of petrochemical plastics, now universally used—there is no country where plastics are not utilized in one form or another. However, most people never give much thought about their disposal. Shopping bags, food containers, food-storage bags, utensils, and plastics in industrial products are all dumped into landfills or directly into rivers and oceans. The discovery by scientists of five large regions of nation-sized "gyres" of plasticized waters in the world's oceans is a tremendous tragedy. These small particles of plastic are swallowed by fish and other marine life, resulting in death. This should be a wake-up call to completely rethink the materials that we use and the manner in which they are recycled. Greenpeace and other organizations are working to highlight and solve the problem.

Developed countries have extremely rigid and high food safety standards for slaughterhouses, agricultural farms, and packaging and storing food. Grocery chains have stringent quality controls for the food and produce they sell. There are stringent standards for the production, pasteurization, and sale of milk. When it comes to garbage and industrial waste, we need far more stringent standards than those for foods. We do not have the right to trash this planet by dumping waste indiscriminately. We are passing on painful legacies to future generations—mountains of garbage, plasticized oceans, and other industrial waste that we produce in exponentially increasing quantities.

We must switch to a system of perfect waste management. Every item that does not biodegrade has no place in landfills and must not be indiscriminately dumped into the environment. Where garbage is bagged in liners made of petrochemical plastics and dumped into landfills, what looks like a clean method of disposing waste from homes and commercial establishments actually provides little thought for end results. Clearly we need to change these unacceptable practices. With the availability of biodegradable plastics from plant sources, legislation should ensure a slow but gradual change from the use of petrochemical plastics in products that collectively end up in landfills to biodegradable plastics. We need to fund research in new technologies for the collection and recycling of products that do not biodegrade. It should be easily possible to have automated systems of identifying and sorting waste products in designated containers that are automatically streamed into different paths for disposal in landfills or to be recycled.

Change will come from educating our children, who more easily embrace such initiatives. Families in any society I have visited take a great deal of pride in keeping their homes clean and tidy. This planet is our home, and housekeeping is a collective responsibility we all share. The goal to maintain a clean and beautiful planet must be a global effort. We need an entirely new approach to the important albeit unpleasant task of being better managers of the disposal of the millions of tons of garbage and waste products that we generate every day.

Regeneration of Our Planet

In one of my visits to a national park in India several years ago, I found an extremely beautiful sign posted on its premises: "Nature has enough for our needs, but not enough for our greed."

I was pleasantly surprised by this perceptive observation, a beautiful piece of wisdom of whose authorship I am unsure. It is painfully obvious in the year 2014 that nature does not have enough even for our needs.

We must regulate the global fishing industry and restock oceans, rivers, and lakes on a global scale. We have always viewed the oceans as an inexhaustible source of food. However, as we deplete the capacity of oceans to sustain populations of fish, with resulting dwindling catches, we need a gigantic global operation to restock the world's waters. It may sound ridiculous, but there is no other option unless we are willing to accept oceans, rivers, and lakes that have been emptied of most of their natural inhabitants. As long as we are dependent on harvesting the oceans for food, we need to better regulate the global fishing industry and work to restore the oceans to the pristine state that existed for millions of years.

Deforestation is another global phenomenon that has accelerated over the past few centuries. The consequences have been catastrophic, with rains washing away topsoil, frequent flooding, and effects on climate change, not to mention the countless species of animals being driven to extinction. Regulation of the global timber industry and reforestation are both needed on an urgent basis.

If we can manufacture a majority of the world's nutritional needs in large factories by synthetic means, the need for harvesting the oceans for food and the use of land for cattle and crops would dwindle. So while we attempt to develop synthetic foods we need to embark both on a massive global restocking program of the oceans and on a reforestation program of vast tracts of land that have been stripped of their forests. This would permit us to regenerate the planet.

The key to success is to bring together a large number of experts in these fields in a global coalition, provide the funding they need, and develop clear plans to achieve these goals. A collaborative global effort could reverse our destruction of these two major natural treasures.

Global Health and Wellness Reform

In the year 2014, what is the greatest human health tragedy of our times? The answer is preventable disease. In the less developed countries of the world, infectious diseases continue to be widespread. Typhoid, cholera, malaria, dysentery, poliomyelitis, and tuberculosis—in addition to a large number of other infectious diseases that should have been eliminated from this planet in the last century—continue to sicken and kill millions. In affluent countries, people suffer from illnesses directly related to poor eating habits, sedentary lifestyles, cigarette smoking, and other lifestyle factors, resulting in an epidemic of obesity in children and adults, diabetes, high blood pressure, heart disease, and joint diseases. In the most educated population groups on this planet, a basic ignorance about adopting a healthy lifestyle, maintaining an ideal weight, and preventing diseases of excess has painful consequences. Affluent populations in less developed countries exhibit exactly the same problems. Hence whether we look at underdeveloped countries or the most technologically advanced affluent nations, preventable diseases are the leading causes of human disease and death. As a cardiologist I can emphatically state that every heart attack is a preventable tragedy. The youngest patient I have treated for a heart attack was eighteen years old; he started smoking when he was eleven. I have seen quite a few patients with heart attacks and coronary artery disease in their twenties; with patients in their thirties or forties—I lost count a long time ago.

I maintain that the most important strategies for improving global health and freedom from disease are the following:

1. Prevention
2. Prevention
3. Prevention

As industrialized nations of the world deal with aging populations, expenditures on providing health care to their citizens are fast approaching levels that cannot be sustained. If we are to reduce the burden of disease in poor and rich countries and reduce global expenditures on health care, we will need aggressive disease prevention and wellness programs. The global burden of disease must be dramatically reduced. No magical cures are needed. We have the tools to achieve this.

Prevention consists of two important elements: health education, and visits to health-care professionals.

There is a need for global programs of health education. Ignorance about disease causation, unwillingness to adopt healthy lifestyles, and failure to utilize health-care services for wellness and health promotion are major tragedies. Health education must start in elementary school and continue through high school and college. If we are not going to educate our children on how to lead a healthy lifestyle, how to prevent diseases, the injurious consequences of cholesterol excess, smoking, alcohol, and drugs, then we cannot truly expect them to be enlightened about health. In underdeveloped nations, basic information about preventing infectious diseases, the importance of immunization and sanitation, and the utilization of health-care services is critical. Flavored, carbonated, sugar syrup (carbonated drinks, soda pop) and high-cholesterol foods are the "cigarettes" of the twenty-first century. They are widely marketed and sold as lifestyle foods. Without true knowledge of their dangers, very large population groups ingest them in great quantities, leading to obesity, juvenile and adult diabetes, and premature coronary artery disease. Because they are "foods," they are hard to regulate. The only effective counterforce is excellent health education. The food industry bombards children and adults with aggressive marketing campaigns that are not matched by the wisdom of the true facts needed to make informed choices. Worldwide, an almost complete absence in the curriculum of the subjects of wellness, human disease and its causation, and disease prevention leaves children with no reliable source to obtain such knowledge. We need not merely career preparation but lifelong health and wellness preparation. Materials developed specifically for every country or region must impart a comprehensive health education.

The second half of disease prevention is the adoption of visits to health professionals and health-care centers for wellness and health promotion. Can we mandate periodic health-care visits for citizens of a nation? This would be a controversial strategy; hence, excellent education and online resources are probably more likely to work. In many countries health examinations are mandatory for school children, and immunizations need to be current due to the risk of spreading infectious diseases. Yet once past high school and college, health-care visits are no longer compulsory. The origins of a large number of diseases that occur in middle-aged population groups and seniors can often be found at an early age. Ill patients would obviously require frequent visits. However, for all adults, health-care visits at least every five years would detect diseases early, monitor health, and provide health and wellness information. We need to shift the paradigm from going to a doctor when one is unwell to going to a doctor when one is in good health, to maintain one's health and prevent the occurrence of disease. This is a lesson taught in medical schools for the past few decades, yet poorly adopted by most nations.

Programs at the national and global levels must be adequately funded by government agencies or health-insurance companies, and legislation should be based on the design of excellent programs. All wellness and health promotion programs should be free or markedly subsidized to the user. There may be value in considering nationwide networks of free clinics to facilitate this and health insurance plans that make such visits free. With several different models of health-care delivery in different countries, there will be no uniform model. However the principle must be that preventative health measures should be provided free or at subsidized rates to every citizen. A massive media campaign, coupled with imparting true knowledge and awareness of health and wellness, could control spiraling global health-care costs. Only investments in prevention programs can reduce the burden of disease and lead to healthy and productive citizens.

Clean Water

Every human being on this planet should have access to clean water. Clean water is a basic need. If we are to eradicate a variety of waterborne illnesses, ensuring clean water is a fundamental strategy. Although developed countries may not perceive it as a major issue, in underdeveloped countries safe drinking water is an immense need for every community. If we accept this as a global goal, then we can identify the resources that are needed.

A few tragedies exacerbate the scarcity of clean water: often violence stands in the way in the very nations where the need is greatest; an exploding population dwarfs the supplies that are available; and funds to embark on ambitious projects are limited. Every nation's strategy will be different. Even in developed countries, periodic droughts lead to a scarcity of drinking water and devastating effects on agricultural crops dependent on rainwater for irrigation. Using groundwater for irrigation means a dropping of the water tables, leading to difficulties in food production.

All countries need water-treatment plants, and we need to find the funding so that every human has access to clean water for domestic use. Stable and secure supplies of water for both domestic use and for irrigation require exploring options that constitute a major paradigm shift from the current status quo. The oceans are a single large repository of water on this planet. Drinking water and water for irrigation needs can be substantially met by gigantic desalination plants in countries bordering the oceans. In 2014,

our agriculture seems to be as dependent on seasonal rain-
fall as primitive civilizations were. The natural process of
the evaporation of water from the oceans to be carried in
moisture-bearing clouds to rain on land is a gigantic process
of natural desalination. Nature must serve as the model for
assuring unlimited water supplies to meet the needs of the
burgeoning human population.

In the United States, very large investments estab-
lished a system of roads and highways that link every town
and city. The high-quality system of interstate highways
provides for a reliable mode of transportation of goods
and fuel from ports and harbors to every city and town. In
a similar fashion, I can easily visualize gigantic desalination plants bordering the oceans with pipelines to pump
water not only for domestic use but also as an assured
supply for irrigation. We need breakthrough desalination
technologies that will make this an economically viable
strategy. Abundant and cheap clean water extracted from
the oceans could allow conversion of large drought-prone
areas into agricultural land. Croplands that depend on rain
could potentially have an assured supply of water for irrigation, leading to stability in food production. Desalination
technology can benefit a great many countries across the
world. Just as generating electricity in power plants and
distributing it on national grids has been applied glob-
ally, networks of behemoth desalination plants, pumping
stations, canals, and pipelines could provide water across
nations, especially to the neediest areas. Lakes that have
dried out because of drought or unregulated drainage
could be refilled.

If the majority of human nutritional needs were met by synthesized foods, then one of the greatest needs for water—to irrigate croplands would be substantially reduced. The water saved could be diverted for domestic and industrial needs. Hence a major change in our sourcing and supply of water also depends on breakthroughs in other fields.

Clean water is a fundamental need that begs for global resources to address it effectively. Clean water is also linked to peace and stability in drought-stricken nations. Until we have a multifaceted, comprehensive plan, where each goal is achieved, we will never reach a lasting solution. Yet the provisioning of adequate clean water for every need is easily within our grasp. All we lack is the vision and resources to achieve this goal.

NO PRICE IS TOO HIGH

Funding and Powering Critical Global Initiatives

For any plan to succeed in practically any field of human endeavor, it almost always depends on adequate funding. The plans and goals outlined in this book will be merely interesting thoughts without the resources to actualize them. Large-scale global plans need funding from governments supplemented by private funding. Such global investments depend on moving away from armed conflict, developing a federation of nations committed to peace, and diverting funds currently used for military preparedness to peaceful, developmental initiatives. The wars in Iraq and Afghanistan cost over one trillion dollars. Violence, whether in occupying neighboring countries, as an ideological tool in preparation for dealing with perceived enemies, or in the implied threat of using weapons of mass destruction has predictable consequences. No militarily strong nation with a robust economy will tolerate such lethal initiatives. Throughout history, nations have prioritized military strength and the protection of their own citizens and borders. How do we renounce violence and still prevent such lethal provocations in the future? The answer is a federation of democracies that is inclusive, respectful of all religions and cultures, and wedded to peace and productive developmental efforts. The might of such an organization and the progressive inclusion of every country on this planet should do away with the threat of large-scale global wars or acts of terrorism.

Changing from thousands of years of wars, conflict, and military preparedness to a peaceful productive coexistence will never be easy. Yet doing so is the pressing need of our times. Too many global development plans fail for lack of funding. Affluent nations see little reason to fund developmental efforts in countries around the world that are ideologically antagonistic to them. Severe drought, floods, earthquakes, or epidemics do activate nations to help. However, for basic developmental programs in many critical areas, nations have little enthusiasm to come forward with such funds. With an economic downturn in most economies of the world, the possibility of large amounts of money being made available as aid is extremely unlikely. Hence the first step is to develop a coalition of democratic nations that are permanent members of such an enlightened group. By guaranteeing peace, stability, and a long-term partnership, the possibility of nations investing in developmental efforts in such a coalition increases substantially.

An important source of funding could be a global tax on goods and services to raise the monies needed. In an age of economic crisis, such a proposal may be difficult to support. However, let us look at this from an entirely different perspective: During World War II, men and women were called to serve, as the war was fought for a free world. The risk of dying or being injured was real. Today we need to wage a war to save this planet. We need to wage a war to turn humanity from the destructive course on which we have put this planet. We need to wage a war to return this planet to being a paradise for all forms of life for millions of years. If we look at the enormity of the consequences of this large issue, why would we not want to fund a global effort? A global sales tax on all goods and services would probably cover most of the necessary costs. The gross world product (GWP) was around $71.83 trillion in 2012. Should we not dedicate at least two trillion dollars every year for global development efforts? Two trillion per year for the first five years, gradually reduced depending on actual needs, would likely cover the costs for most of the critical programs.

Funding from philanthropic foundations and donations from individuals and corporations also have a critical role to play. For specific programs with clear goals, private giving could be the catalyst for change. Let us take a hypothetical program: zero population growth by the year 2030 (ZPG 2030). The program would build a global network of standalone free clinics and would staff additional program personnel in existing clinics, primary health centers, and hospitals worldwide. It would focus on nations or regions with explosive population growth rates. Education about contraception and family planning with a media blitz and online resources would launch in tandem with free contraceptives and family-planning services. Empowering women is the key to success. Permanent methods of contraception should be encouraged, and in many countries financial incentives and tax benefits may help. There is no reason why the ZPG 2030 program cannot buy out or start companies that manufacture contraceptives, mass produce such products, and provide them free at networks of clinics and hospitals. Effective methods of contraception have been available for decades; however, we lack vision, a global plan, and a trailblazing organization to lead the way. Such a ZPG 2030 program would be an ideal one for private foundations and the wealthiest of the wealthy to launch, coordinate, and execute, coordinating its efforts with the WHO and governmental and nongovernmental agencies. I believe that it is easily possible to achieve this goal by the year 2030.

The wealthiest and most enterprising nations and individuals must take the lead. We need to rise above our trivial differences and urgently focus our energies on plans to tackle our major problems. We can succeed in saving the planet if we rise above our differences, recognize the oneness of all humans and life forms, and work shoulder to shoulder toward clear goals. We do have the power to succeed. We must succeed.

7000 AD

The great pyramids in Egypt were built approximately five thousand years ago. Five thousand years is like the blink of an eye on a planet that is 4.5 billion years old. Unless some natural disaster makes life on this planet extinct, there will be life on this planet five thousand years from now. Let us ask ourselves a rhetorical question: What will the future hold for Earth's inhabitants in 7000 AD? I foresee two distinct and very different scenarios.

The first scenario has been predicted by numerous experts over the past several decades. If we continue on the current path of explosive and uncontrolled population growth and the unbridled growth of polluting technologies, this planet will be pushed over the edge to a living hell. The planet will hold far more humans than it could ever sustain. What will that number be? The exact number can never be predicted with any degree of accuracy. Cities and towns will eat into all the forests we have. The starving billions will be ripe for decimation due to famine or disease. The oceans will have trivial amounts of marine life. Global warming will reach intolerable levels. Flooding of the current major population centers along the coasts will lead to mass migrations. Vast areas of farmlands will be converted into dustbowls. Billions will lack clean water. The infrastructure of roads and transportation will slowly crumble. Incessant wars and conflict will result in recurrent spasms of violence that will ripple through major population centers. Innumerable species of plant and animal life will become extinct. None of those prospects is an exaggeration but instead a reasonable forecast—and one we may reach in far less than a thousand years. That is the path we now apathetically walk on, despite the mountains of scientific knowledge and warnings from innumerable experts urging otherwise. That is where this path will lead us.

The second scenario is what I fervently hope we will achieve: I can clearly see in the millennia ahead human beings becoming an enlightened and wise species. I can clearly see a time when conflict, wars, and violence will be only a part of this planet's past. I can see a time when a peace-loving species will consider its most important role to be wise custodians of this planet, to nurture it and serve as shepherds of all living creatures. Amazing technological breakthroughs that we cannot even contemplate today will help. However, all technologies will be governed by the principle of being able to nurture the planet and not destroy it.

I can clearly see the population of humans gradually being reduced to less than one billion. Massive reforestation programs resulting in most of the land being reforested and green. Oceans restocked and brimming with marine life. Food being manufactured in huge, green factories. A time when the entire planet draws its energy needs from completely green sources of energy. A time when humans have learned to be equal members of a global community wedded to peace, prosperity, and knowledge. A species engaged in exploring the universe far outside the reaches of our own solar system and unlocking the mysteries of the universe to benefit this planet for millions of years into the future.

As a species, our vision is far too narrow and short-sighted at present. We need to rise above our differences and historical prejudices and hatreds. A hundred years from now, almost 100 percent of the humans that now walk this planet, with very few exceptions, will be dead. In our place will walk children who are yet to be born. Hence for us to succeed as a species the only thing that truly matters is whether we can leave a legacy that will endure for millions of years into the future. Can we bring all humans into a global community that holds this ideal as one of the most important reasons for our existence? It would require us to break down all the walls that divide us. It would require a great deal of courage. It would require us to hold the simple and obvious fact that "We are the highest form of mammals. We belong to the species *Homo sapiens*" as a truth that transcends all our perceived differences.

The next hundred years is the time to take major steps to stop our destructive ways before we cross the point of no return. My book is written as a plea—a deep, anguished cry to help save our endangered planet. Let us take the time to contemplate these enormous issues and find a way to come together and work to leave behind a beautiful legacy for millions of years to come.